HAL LEONARD

GLOCKENS... ...IOD

A Beginner's Guide with Step-by-Step Instruction for Glockenspiel

BY EVELYN GLENNIE

Photos © Kaupo Kikkas and © Caroline Purday
Videos produced by Made By Berlin Ltd
Audio arranged and recorded by Christopher Hussey

To access audio and video visit:
www.halleonard.com/mylibrary

Enter Code
6711-3631-9719-9982

ISBN 978-1-70517-579-8

Visit Hal Leonard Online at
www.halleonard.com

World headquarters, contact:
Hal Leonard
7777 West Bluemound Road
Milwaukee, WI 53213
Email: info@halleonard.com

In Europe, contact:
Hal Leonard Europe Limited
1 Red Place
London, W1K 6PL
Email: info@halleonardeurope.com

In Australia, contact:
Hal Leonard Australia Pty. Ltd.
4 Lentara Court
Cheltenham, Victoria, 3192 Australia
Email: info@halleonard.com.au

PREFACE ▶️

I first started playing the glockenspiel at school when I was 12 years old. I love this instrument; it is small, you can stand up or sit down to play it, and it is capable of producing a wonderful array of different sounds. It can also be played either on its own or in combination with many other instruments. Just like its gleaming bars, the sound of a glockenspiel really sparkles, so it can cut through a huge orchestra or powerful rock band.

The glockenspiel is the perfect instrument on which to begin a musical journey. It is accessible, rewarding, and provides plenty of scope for stretch and challenge. Plus, it sounds great playing all different styles of music, from classical favorites to pop hits or modern art music. The glockenspiel can open up a world of dynamics, articulation, and general musicianship that will foster a love for music-making and apply seamlessly to the learning of other instruments. It can also act as a gateway to performing in ensembles, from percussion groups to bands and orchestras. Music is an art form whose medium is sound and it can be created from anything: our voices, our bodies, nature, musical instruments, or even machinery! Just as a chef creates a scrumptious meal from food for us to eat, a musician creates an amazing meal from sound. In this book, you will be the musician, creating wonderful sound-meals from the glockenspiel.

Evelyn

Evelyn Glennie, 2022

HOW TO USE THIS BOOK

In this book, the reader will learn the basics of how to play the glockenspiel through a series of meticulously graded pieces of music, composed by Evelyn Glennie. Each piece is carefully sequenced, allowing the user to progressively develop new skills and build upon previous learning. Including elements such as posture, technique, and music reading, this method will work equally well for individual or group learning.

This book is packed full of tutorial videos, making learning more effective and enjoyable. Demonstration and backing tracks are included in the price of this book. Stream or download using the unique code found on page 1. Includes **PLAYBACK+**, a multi-functional audio player that allows you to slow down audio without changing pitch, set loop points, change keys, and pan left or right – available exclusively from Hal Leonard.

ABOUT THE AUTHOR

Dame Evelyn Glennie is the first person in history to create and sustain a full-time career as a solo percussionist, performing worldwide with the greatest orchestras and artists. Evelyn paved the way for orchestras globally to feature percussion concerti when she played the first percussion concerto in the history of the BBC Proms at the Royal Albert Hall, London in 1992.

A leading commissioner of new music, Evelyn has commissioned over 200 works from many of the world's most eminent composers. Evelyn composes music for film, television, and theatre. She is a double GRAMMY® Award winner and BAFTA nominee. She regularly provides masterclasses and consultations to inspire the next generation of musicians. Her film *Touch the Sound*, TED Talk, and book *Listen World!* are key testimonies to her unique and innovative approach to sound-creation.

Leading 1,000 drummers, Evelyn had a prominent role in the opening ceremony of the London 2012 Olympic Games, which also featured a new instrument, the "Glennie Concert Aluphone." Evelyn's solo recordings currently exceed 40 albums and range from original improvisations, collaborations, percussion concerti, and ground-breaking modern solo percussion projects.

Evelyn was awarded an OBE in 1993 and now has over 100 international awards to date, including the "Polar Music Prize" and the "Companion of Honour." She was recently appointed the first female President of Help Musicians, only the third person to hold the title since Sir Edward Elgar and Sir Peter Maxwell Davies. Since 2021, she has been Chancellor of Robert Gordon University, Aberdeen, Scotland.

Evelyn is curator of "The Evelyn Glennie Collection," which includes in excess of 3,500 percussion instruments. Through her mission to "Teach the World to Listen," she aims to improve communication and social cohesion by encouraging everyone to discover new ways of listening in order to inspire, create, engage, and empower.

CONTENTS

YOUR GLOCKENSPIEL

The glockenspiel is a **pitched** percussion instrument, which means it can play musical notes (**pitches**). Glockenspiels come in all different shapes, sizes, and colors. Broadly speaking, there are two types: **framed** and **desktop**. Framed glockenspiels are fixed onto a frame and you play them standing up. Desktop glockenspiels can be placed inside a hard case, on the floor, or on a table or keyboard stand. You can play them standing up or seated. Either type is fine for this book.

FRAMED GLOCKENSPIEL

DESKTOP GLOCKENSPIEL

To play all the music in this book (and most glockenspiel music generally), you will need a **chromatic** glockenspiel with at least 23 glockenspiel bars. A chromatic glockenspiel has two rows of bars, similar to a piano keyboard. The top row of bars are like the black piano keys. The bottom row of bars are like the white piano keys.

The shorter the bar, the higher the pitch

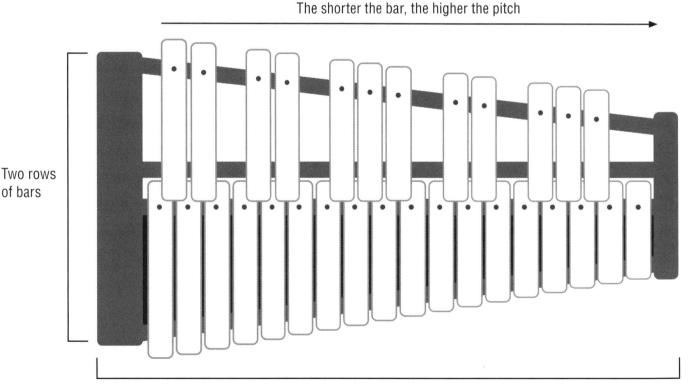

Two rows of bars

Minimum of 23 bars

PARTS OF THE GLOCKENSPIEL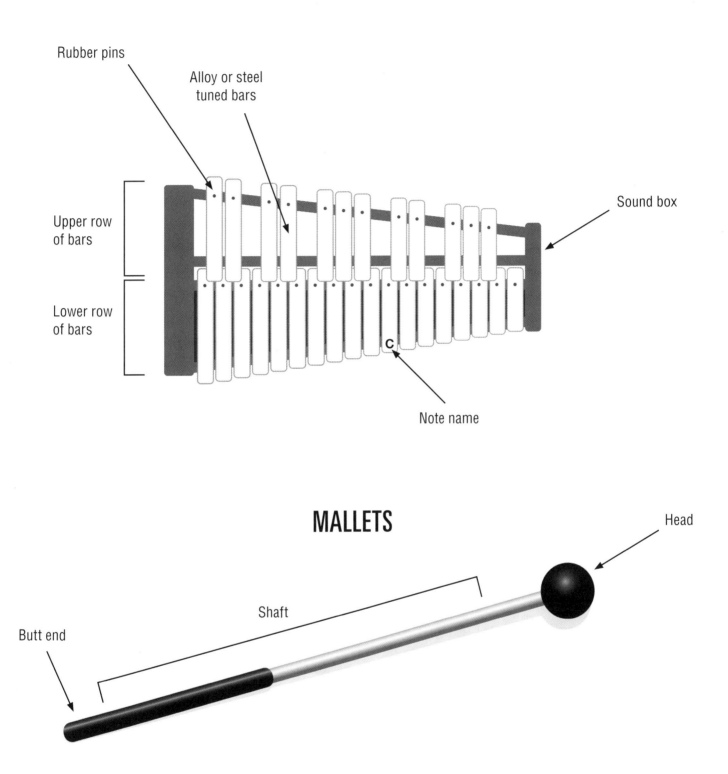

Rubber pins

Alloy or steel
tuned bars

Sound box

Upper row
of bars

Lower row
of bars

c

Note name

MALLETS

Head

Shaft

Butt end

Glockenspiel bars are struck with **mallets**. (They can also be called
"sticks," "beaters," or "hammers.")

Mallets can come in different shapes, lengths, and materials
(including rubber, plastic, glass, wood, brass, latex, and yarn).
Each mallet produces a different type of sound on the glockenspiel.

GETTING READY TO PLAY

POSITIONING AND POSTURE ▶

- A desktop glockenspiel can be placed on any flat, stable surface such as a desk, table, or the floor.

- It is important to keep the instrument completely flat and level so that the position of playing is consistent.

- If sitting to play the glockenspiel on the floor, raise it to a height that allows you to have a straight back and free arm movement. Avoid slouching and rigidly pointing out your elbows.

- When standing to play, make sure that your glockenspiel is not lower than waist height and your arms are at a 90-degree angle when striking the bars. This will allow you to have free but controlled movement.

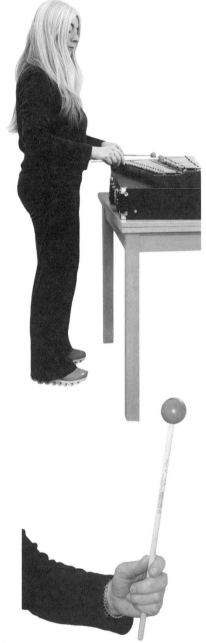

HOLDING THE MALLETS ▶

- Hold the mallets with both right and left hands from the outset.

- Find a natural, comfortable holding area along the shaft of the mallet, perhaps three-quarters towards the butt end.

- Very lightly wrap the fingers around so that the mallets can be free to move gently within the hand. Use your thumb to support the outside of the mallet and wrap your index finger around the other side. This finger should not be on top of the mallet. Move the remaining fingers under your index finger. Imagine that the mallets are an extension of your arms and hands, keeping your grip nice and relaxed.

TAKING CARE OF HEARING

As the sound of the glockenspiel is high and resonant, it is important to avoid playing too loudly for long periods. Using softer mallets is recommended for extended playing. It is fine to use ear protection, too.

STICKING

It's important in music to count a steady **beat**. The beat is what you tap along to when listening to a song. It is like your pulse or the ticking of a clock.

A **whole note** has a beat count of four. 𝅝

When we see a whole note, we count "1, 2, 3, 4": steady and regular.

We **strike** (hit) the glockenspiel bars using mallets in both hands. Underneath the whole notes are the letters "R" and "L." These letters tell us which hand to use. This is called **sticking**. In this piece, there are four different sticking patterns for you to try.

L = Left Hand   **R = Right Hand**

Find a "C" bar to strike for this piece. To help, the letter is written inside the noteheads on the music. The C bar is usually immediately to the left of the group of two bars on the top row.

Here We Go! 🔊

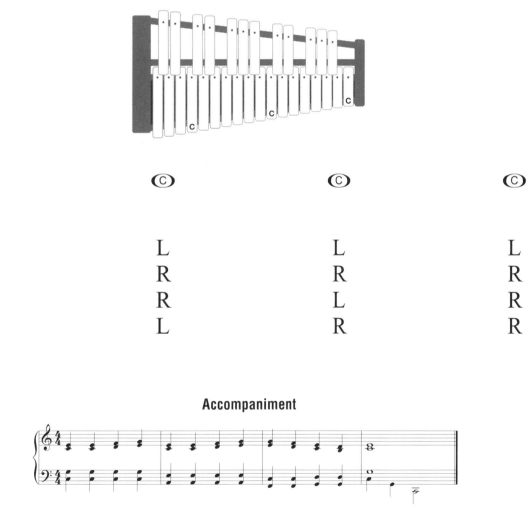

Ⓒ	Ⓒ	Ⓒ	Ⓒ
L	L	L	L
R	R	R	R
L	R	L	R
R	L	R	R

Accompaniment

EVELYN'S TIPS

- Remember to very lightly wrap the fingers around the mallets. Let them freely drop to the bar before returning straight back up.
- The sound from both your right and left hands should be of **equal** strength and purity.

NEW NOTES: D, E, F, AND G

Measure

Bar lines divide the music up into **measures**, making it easier to read.

At the end of a piece of music, we have a **terminal double bar line**.

Still using whole notes and counting "1, 2, 3, 4," we are now going to practice moving up and down the glockenspiel, striking five bars. In this piece, we are moving to bars that are right next to each other. This is called moving by **step**.

Start on any "C" to play this piece as long as you have enough room to go up by step five bars to "G." To help, the note names that correspond to the glockenspiel bars are written inside the noteheads. You can use the glockenspiel diagram above the music as a guide, too. Practice using the four different sticking patterns suggested below.

Stepping Stones

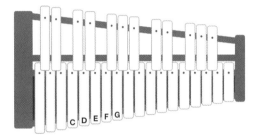

C	D	E	F	G	F	E	D	C
L	L	L	L	L	L	L	L	L
R	R	R	R	R	R	R	R	R
L	R	L	R	L	R	L	R	L
R	L	R	L	R	L	R	L	R

Accompaniment

10

NEW RHYTHMS

THE HALF NOTE

A **half note** is a note value that gets two beat counts: "1, 2." There are two half notes in a whole note.
In this piece, we are going to count half notes, striking the same bars as we did for "Stepping Stones."

Helping Hand

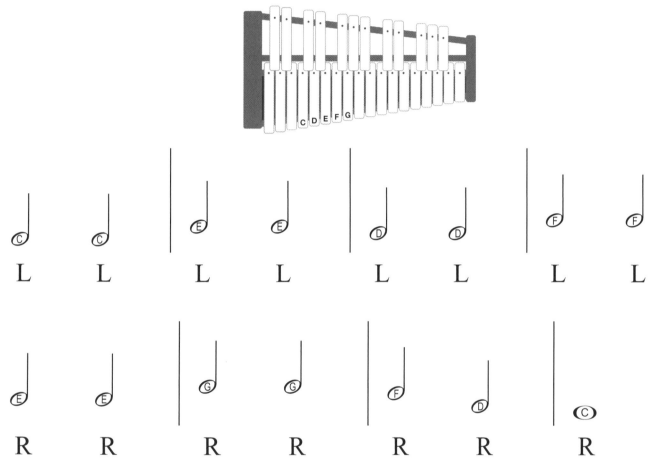

Accompaniment

TWO NEW NOTES: A AND B

Let's now play music that involves striking the "A" and "B" glockenspiel bars. These are the last remaining note names on the lower row of the glockenspiel and you can see them on the diagram below.

Let's Play "A," Let's Play "B"

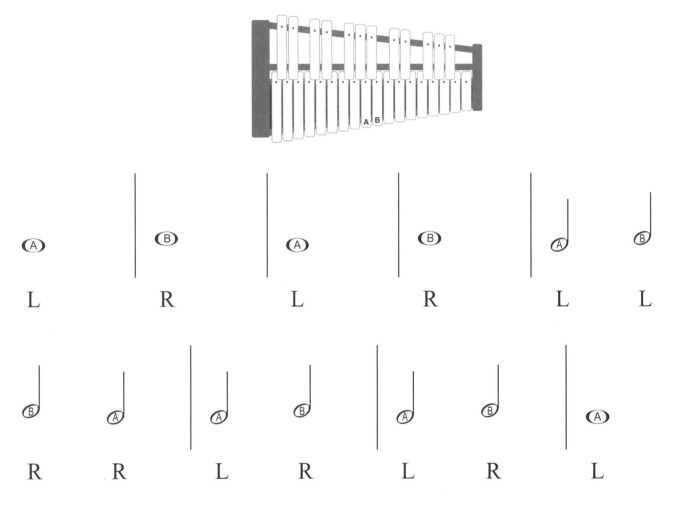

Accompaniment

This Way, That Way

Accompaniment

LEAPING

We now know all the note names on the lower row of the glockenspiel: C, D, E, F, G, A, and B. Have a look at your glockenspiel. Notice that this pattern is repeated throughout the lower row of bars. Once you get to a "B" bar, you go back to "C" and it all starts over again.

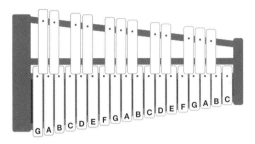

Notice that there are several bars with the same letter name. Bars that have the same letter name sound higher or lower versions of the same note. Here, the circled glockenspiel bars all sound higher and lower versions the note "C." When we strike glockenspiel bars that are far apart, we are **leaping**. Play around with striking all the different "C" bars on your glockenspiel, leaping from one bar to the next.

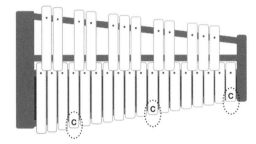

Now, do the same but with the D, E, F, and G glockenspiel bars.

High and Low Ds

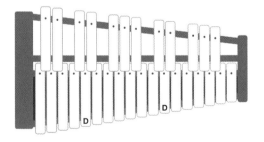

High and Low Fs

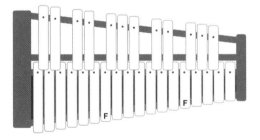

High and Low Es

High and Low Gs

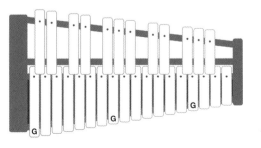

14

LEAPING EXERCISES

Each of the following exercises involves playing the same note but at **two different pitches**: low and high. The low and high versions of the same note are separated by eight lower glockenspiel bars. This is known as an **octave**. Use the diagram above each piece to help.

Short exercises or scales end with a **thin double bar line**.

High C, Low C Drill

High D, Low D Drill

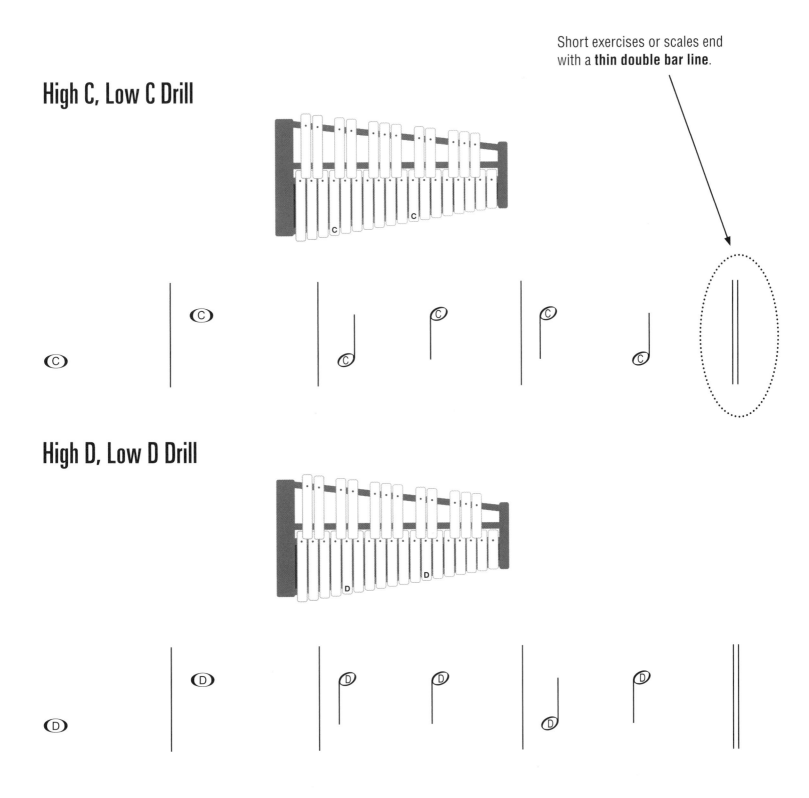

High E, Low E Drill

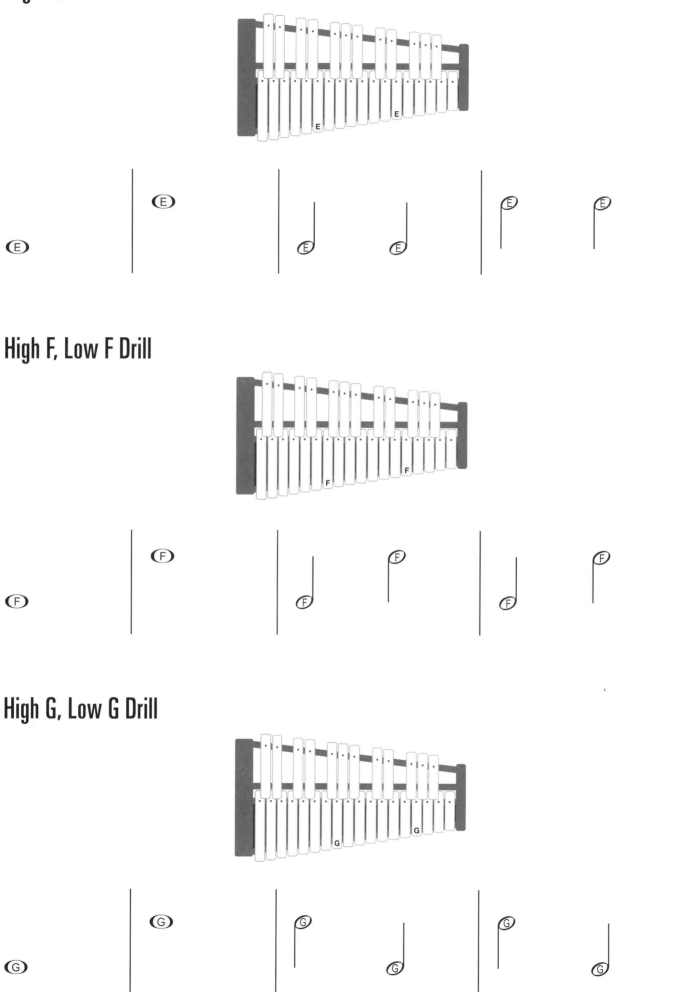

High F, Low F Drill

High G, Low G Drill

NEW RHYTHMS

THE QUARTER NOTE

A **quarter note** is worth one beat. There are two quarter notes in a half note and four quarter notes in a whole note.

We are now going to play the piece "Little Dream." This piece only contains quarter notes and uses all of the pitches we have learned so far.

Little Dream

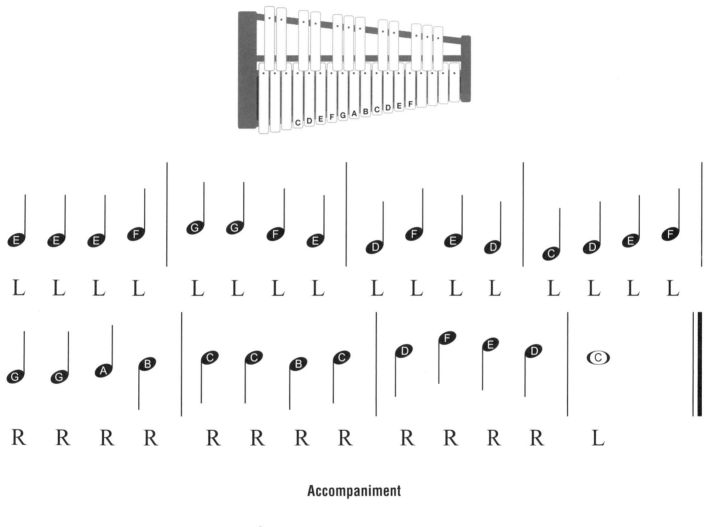

Accompaniment

TIME SIGNATURES

At the start of a piece of music you'll usually see two numbers, one on top of the other. This symbol is known as a **time signature**. It tells us how many beats are in each measure.

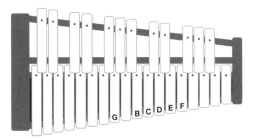

$\frac{4}{4}$ ← Four beats in a measure
    ← The beat is a quarter note

Snowflake 🔊

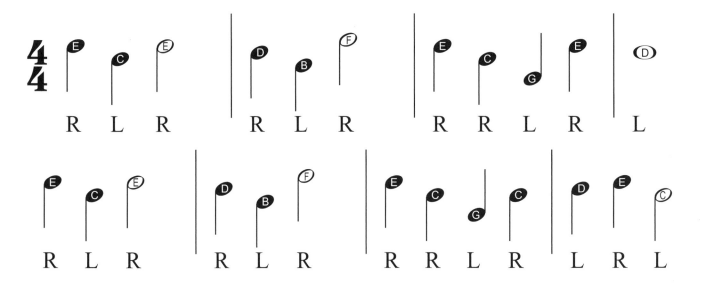

Accompaniment

EVELYN'S TIP

• Once you've mastered the sticking suggested in the music, why not try making up your own?

EXTENDED NOTES

$\frac{2}{4}$ AND THE TIE

A tie is a curved line that joins two note values together. You hold the note for the total number of beats created by the tie.

Two beats in a measure   → $\frac{2}{4}$
The beat is a quarter note   →

1   2   (1   2)

Distant Bells

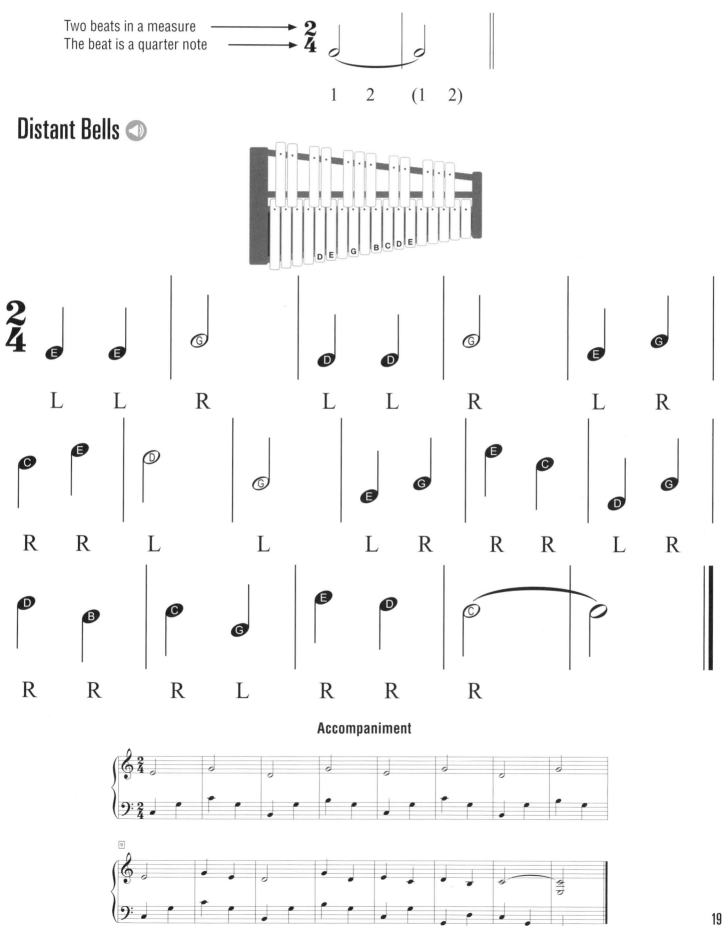

Accompaniment

NEW RHYTHMS

THE DOTTED HALF NOTE AND $\frac{3}{4}$

When you add a dot after a notehead, it increases the value of the note by half.

For a dotted half note, you count three beats.

For this piece, we are going to play in a $\frac{3}{4}$ time signature. This means there are three quarter-note beats in a measure. We count "1, 2, 3."

Dance of the Seahorse

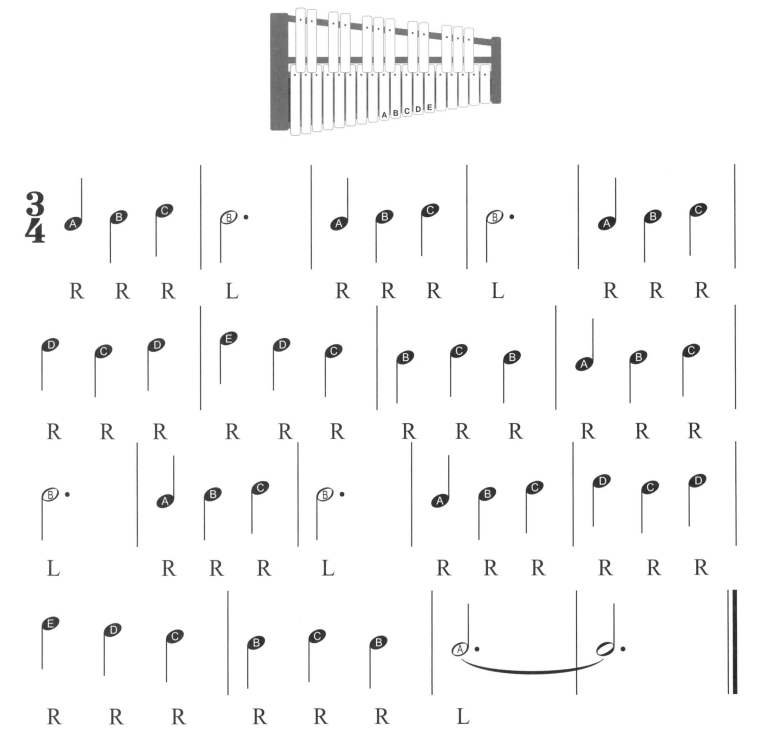

Accompaniment

EIGHTH NOTES

It's time to learn a new note value! An eighth note is half the value of a quarter note. (There are two eighth notes in a quarter note and they are often grouped in pairs by a horizontal **beam**.)

When we play eighth notes, it helps if we count "1-and-2-and-3-and-4-and."

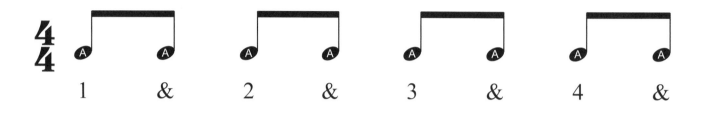

Before we move onto a new piece, here are two exercises that will make counting and playing eighth notes easier.

Eighth-Note Drill 1

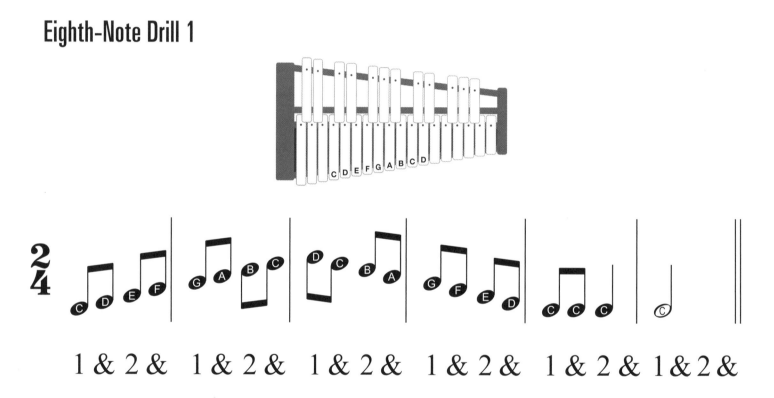

Eighth-Note Drill 2

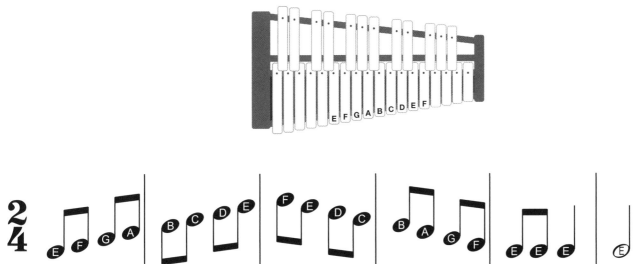

1 & 2 & 1 & 2 & 1 & 2 & 1 & 2 & 1 & 2 & 1 & 2 &

EIGHTH NOTES IN PERFORMANCE

We'll begin by playing a familiar tune. This time, "Dance of the Seahorse" has been adapted to include eighth notes. There are now lots of seahorses dancing around! Play with a smooth, even sound and practice saying the beat count. This will keep you from rushing.

Dance of the Seahorses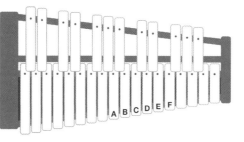

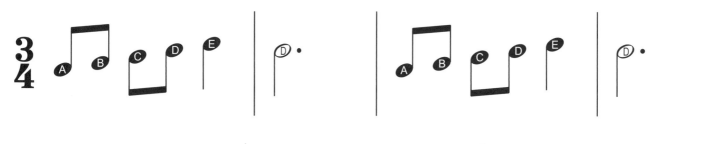

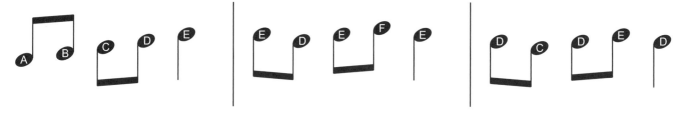

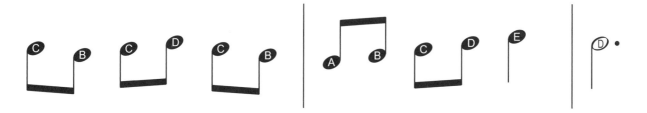

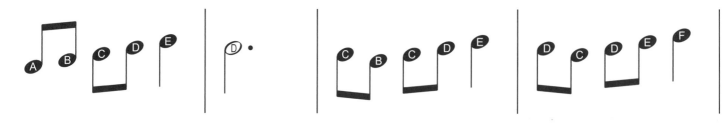

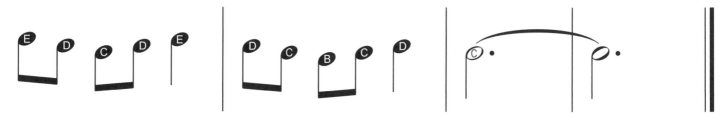

Accompaniment

To and Fro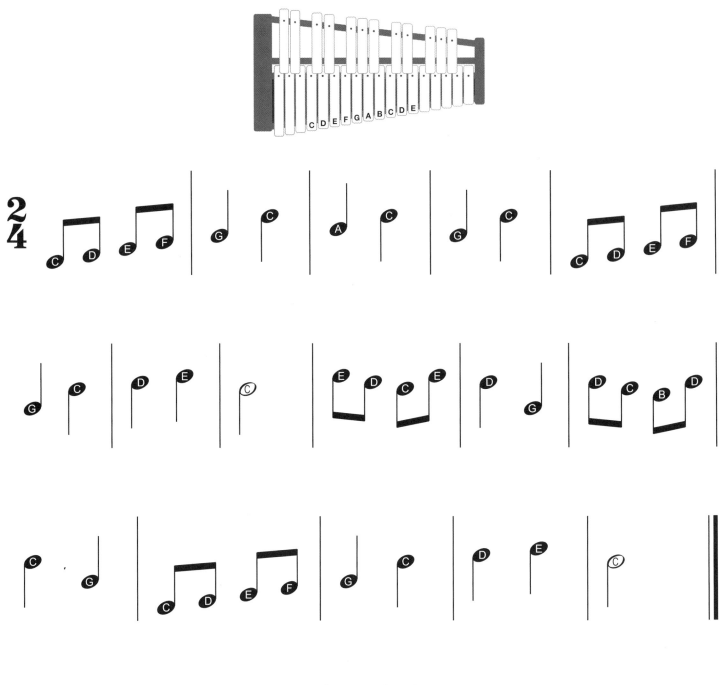

Accompaniment

River Ride

Accompaniment

EVELYN'S TIP

• Holding the mallets in a relaxed way will help you to feel the vibration of the sound as it travels up into your hands.

RESTS

Rests are symbols in music that show us when not to play. Each note value has an equivalent rest symbol, which represents a count of **silence**. You need to count carefully when you see a rest, giving it as much attention as you would a note.

Whole Note and Rest: 𝅝 ▬

Half Note and Rest: 𝅗𝅥 ▬

Quarter Note and Rest: ♩ 𝄽

These two exercises will help you to put the new rest symbols into context. Continue the beat count throughout.

Rest Drill 1

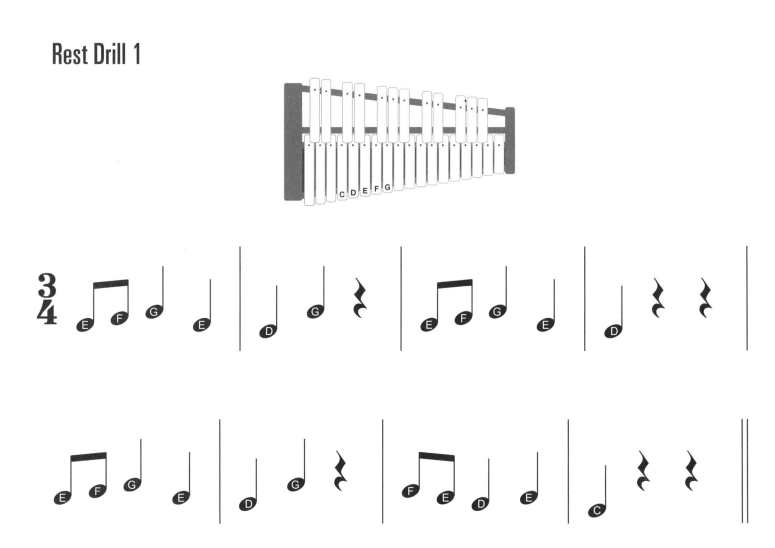

Rest Drill 2

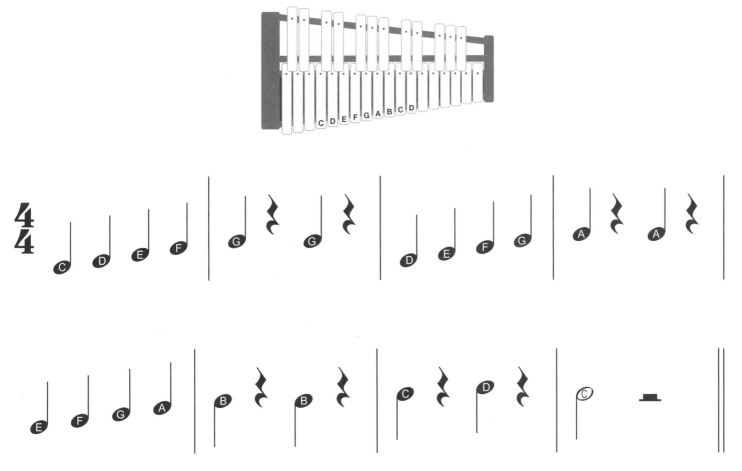

EVELYN'S TIP

• The symbol for a whole rest is also the symbol for an entire measure of silence in any time signature!

THE STAFF

Musical notes are written on a **staff**, which is made up of five lines and four spaces.

Noteheads are placed on the lines or within the spaces of the staff.

At the very beginning of the staff is a symbol known as a **clef**. A clef helps us to identify the names of the notes on the lines and spaces of the staff.

All glockenspiel music uses the **treble clef.**

Here are all the notes we have played so far, represented as whole notes on the treble staff. The music throughout this book is notated two octaves down for ease of reading.

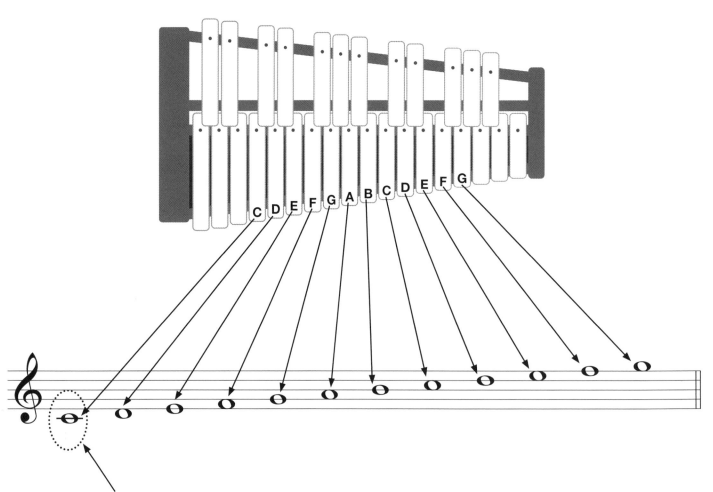

The lowest "C" falls outside of the five staff lines, so it has a little line of its own. This is called a **ledger line**.

C Major Scale

Here is a collection of whole notes on the treble staff. Together, they make up what is known as a **C major scale**. Play each note through, consulting the video for guidance.

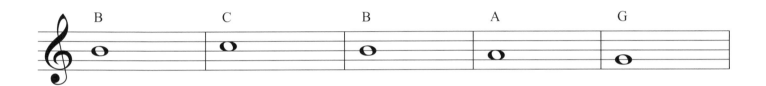

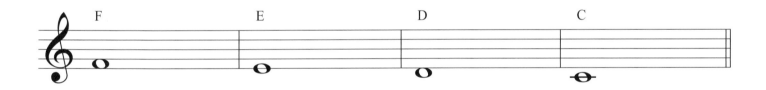

READING MUSIC ON THE STAFF: STEPS

Here are some exercises that will help you to read and play music on the staff. The notes move by **step**. Remember, this means you are striking bars that are right next to each other. You can tell stepwise movement on the staff because the noteheads always move from "line-to-space" or "space-to-line."

Music-Reading Drill: C, D, E

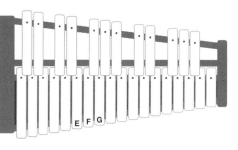

Music-Reading Drill: E, F, G

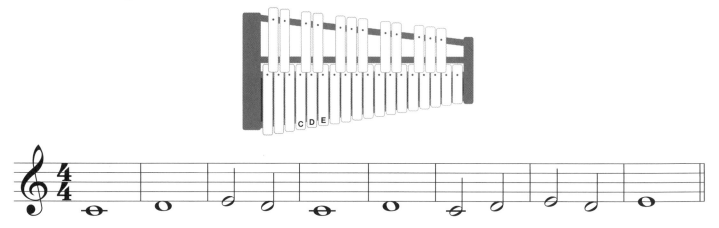

Music-Reading Drill: G, A, B

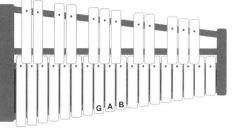

READING MUSIC ON THE STAFF: SKIPS

When notes move from "line-to-line" or "space-to-space" on the staff, we say they are moving in **skips**. This means we strike glockenspiel bars that are not immediately next to one another.

Here are some exercises for reading notes on the staff that move in skips. Note that these exercises use the same letter names but higher-pitched bars than those on page 32.

Music-Reading Drill: C, D, E

Music-Reading Drill: E, F, G

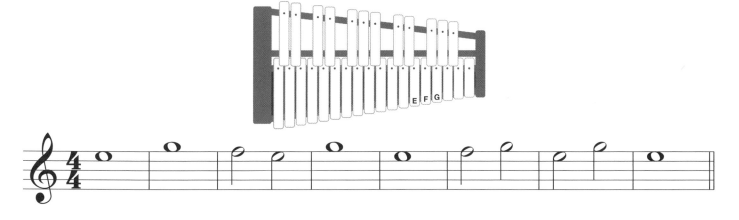

Music-Reading Drill: C–G

NEW RHYTHMS

THE SINGLE EIGHTH NOTE AND EIGHTH REST

Here is the symbol for an **eighth rest**. You count it in exactly the same way as you would do an eighth note. A single eighth note looks like a quarter note with a flag.

Single Eighth Note and Rest: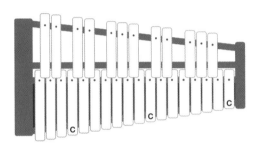

These two eighth-rest exercises will help you to count accurately. Try saying the beat count out loud as you play. You can choose any "C" bar on the glockenspiel to play these drills.

Eighth-Rest Drill 1

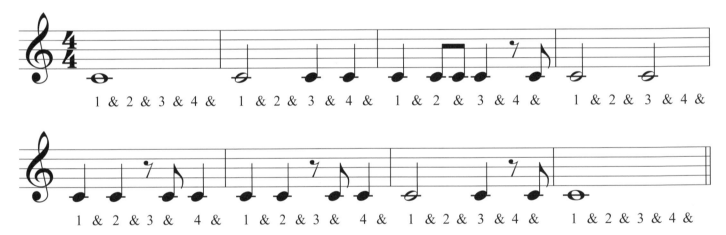

Eighth-Rest Drill 2

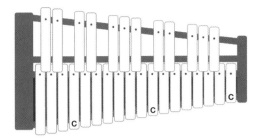

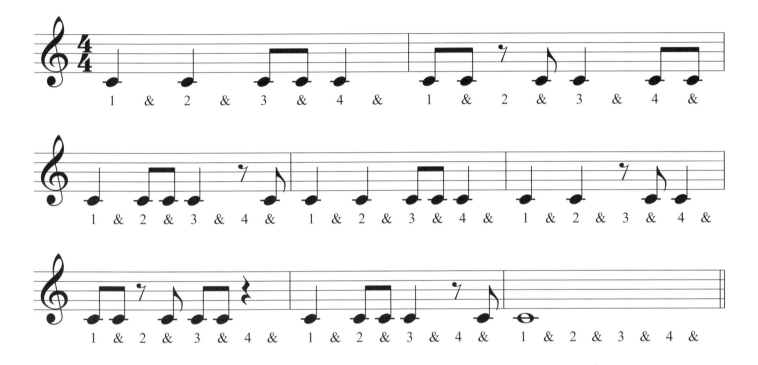

COMBINING NOTES AND RESTS

In this piece, we are going to combine half, quarter, and eighth rests. Count carefully!

Cruising

Accompaniment

STRIKING BARS ON THE TOP ROW

FLATS AND F MAJOR SCALE

A **flat** sign (♭) before a note means to play the very next bar to the left. If a flat appears before a note, it remains for the entire measure.

Sometimes, if a note is flattened for an entire piece, the flat sign appears at the very beginning of the music.

This is known as a **key signature**. It tells us that every time we see a "B" in the music, we must play the "B-flat" bar, located on the top row.

So far, we have been playing using the C major key signature. The key signature with one flat (B-flat) is **F major**.

Here is the F major scale. Starting on F, play up the bottom row of notes. Then, when you reach the note "B" in the music, strike the "B-flat" bar instead. We are playing our top row of glockenspiel bars for the first time!

F G A B♭ C D E F   E D C B♭ A G F

F E D C B♭ A G F   G A B♭ C D E F

EVELYN'S TIP

- Practice this scale thoroughly with alternative sticking and note values until you can move from the bottom to top row of bars and back again smoothly.

PLAYING IN F MAJOR

These pieces are in the key of F major. Can you see the flat sign in the key signature? Before you play, circle all of the "B" notes in the music. This will help to remind you that whenever you see this note, you are going to play the "B-flat" bar on the top row.

Giddy-Up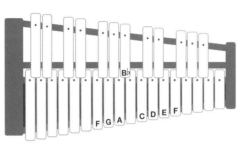

Accompaniment

38

Over and Over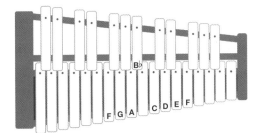

Accompaniment

STRIKING BARS ON THE TOP ROW

SHARPS AND G MAJOR SCALE

A **sharp** sign (♯) before a note means to play the very next bar to the right. If a sharp appears before a note, it remains for the entire measure.

Sometimes, if a note is sharpened for an entire piece, the sharp sign appears at the very beginning of the music.

This tells us that every time we see the note "F" in the music, we must play the "F-sharp" bar. It is the key signature of **G major**.

Here is the G major scale. Starting on G, play up the bottom row of notes. Then, when you reach the note "F" in the music, strike the "F-sharp" bar instead.

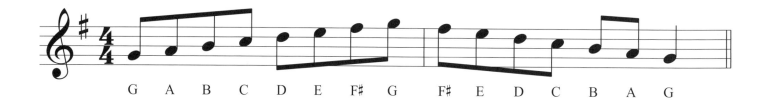

G A B C D E F♯ G F♯ E D C B A G

G F♯ E D C B A G A B C D E F♯ G

PLAYING IN G MAJOR

These pieces are in the key of G major. Can you see the sharp sign in the key signature? Before you play, circle all of the "F" notes in the music. This will help to remind you that whenever you see this note, you are going to play the "F-sharp" bar on the top row.

Give and Take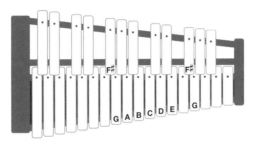

Accompaniment

Together We Sing

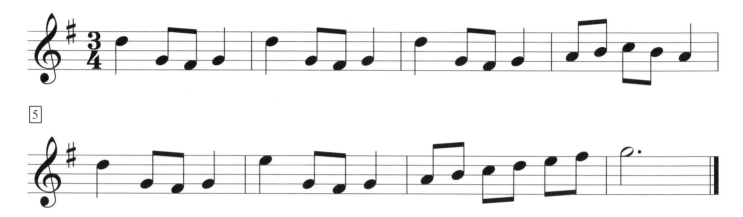

Accompaniment

DYNAMICS

Dynamic markings are symbols that tell us to play loudly, softly, or somewhere in between. Dynamic contrast helps us to put expression into the music that we perform.

f   **Forte** = Strong/Loud

p   **Piano** = Gentle/Soft

mf   **Mezzo Forte** = Moderately Loud

mp   **Mezzo Piano** = Moderately Soft

Bugle Song

Accompaniment

Traveler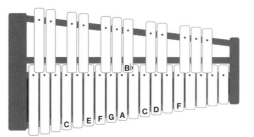

3

6

Accompaniment

EVELYN'S TIPS

- In these two pieces, the music with soft dynamic markings should sound like an echo. Strike the bars lightly but be careful to continue counting a steady beat. Softer does not mean slower!
- Take a careful look at the key signature before you start to play. You might like to circle the notes in the music that you will strike on the top row of your glockenspiel.

HAIRPIN DYNAMICS ▶️

Hairpin dynamics are symbols that tell us to play gradually louder or softer.

Think of hairpin symbols as representing the shape of your mouth.

Imagine saying the words "I am getting louder!" Begin with a whisper and gradually get louder until you are shouting. As you get louder, your mouth gets wider, just like the **crescendo** hairpin.

I am getting louder!

Now, imagine saying the words "I am getting softer." Begin by shouting and gradually get quieter until you end the sentence in a whisper. As you get softer, your mouth gets narrower, just like the **decrescendo** hairpin.

I am getting softer.

Let's play our three scales in eighth notes with hairpin dynamics.

C Major

F Major

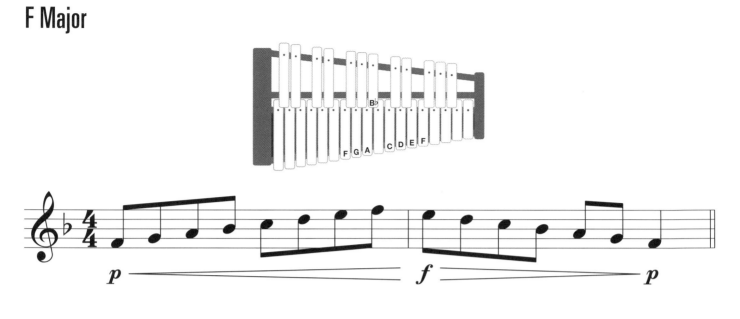

G Major

COMBINING DYNAMIC SYMBOLS

Hairpin Hustle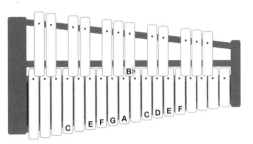

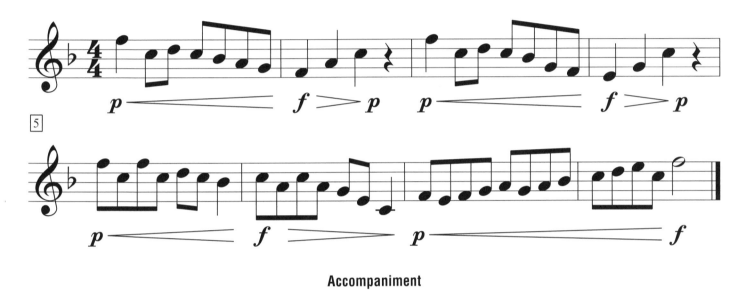

Accompaniment

EVELYN'S TIPS

- Try exaggerating the dynamic markings at first, which will help you to feel the crescendos, decrescendos, and dynamic contrast.
- Be careful to maintain a steady beat count. Be aware that it is tempting to speed up when you get louder and slow down when you get quieter. You could try recording yourself play, listening back to check you are playing to a steady beat. Or you could play to a metronome click. Playing along with the accompaniment tracks will help, too.

Hot 'n' Cold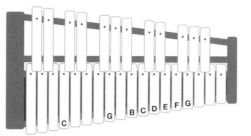

Accompaniment

DEVELOPING MALLET TECHNIQUE

STRENGTH AND FLEXIBILITY

Having equal strength and flexibility in both hands is very important for playing the glockenspiel. Here are two **études** (studies) that will help you to develop these qualities. Practice this first exercise using the following sticking:

- Left hand only

- Right hand only

- Measures 1–2 left hand, measures 3–4 right hand

- Measures 1–2 right hand, measures 3–4 left hand

C Major Étude

F Major Étude

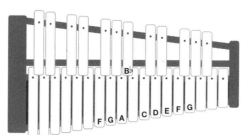

TONE CONTROL

Building on our studies from the previous section, these two pieces isolate the right and left hand. Work on having equal control in both hands, keeping a consistent **tone** (sound quality) regardless of the hand you are using.

Woodpecker Song

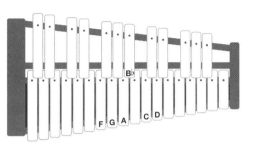

Accompaniment

Trumpet Salute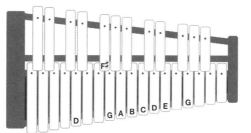

Accompaniment

EVELYN'S TIP

- Keep the hand that is *not* playing hovering above the glockenspiel bars. This ensures that it will be ready to take over smoothly and gracefully. The idea is that we want both hands to be "talking to each other," even if only one is playing.

FLUENT STICKING HANDOVERS

We are now going to play some music to improve the fluency of our sticking handovers. Aim to get these as smooth as possible; a listener should not be able to hear when you move from one hand to another.

Copycat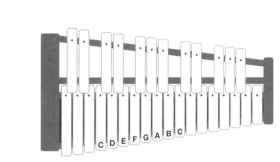

Accompaniment

Let's play "Copycat" once more but change the sticking at every measure. Again, aim for smooth handovers, ensuring that there is no inconsistency in tone quality.

Copycat II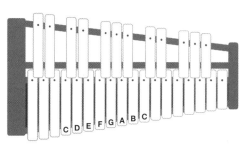

Accompaniment

DOUBLE STOPS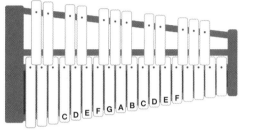

With our hands becoming stronger and more flexible, it is time to introduce **double stops**. A double stop is when two notes are played at exactly the same time. Your left and right hands will strike the bars simultaneously.

Let's start by playing our three major scales in double stops: slowly and steadily, with both hands beautifully coordinated.

C Major Double-Stop Scale

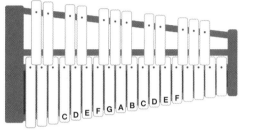

F Major Double-Stop Scale

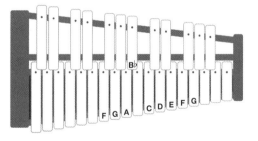

G Major Double-Stop Scale

DOUBLE STOPS IN PERFORMANCE

Hand in Hand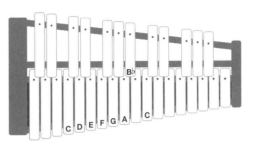

Accompaniment

Can You Hear Me?

EVELYN'S TIP

• Focus on striking the double stops completely together by practicing at first without the dynamic markings.

HAND INDEPENDENCE

Hand independence refers to the technique of glockenspiel playing where both hands are playing different notes and rhythms.

Developing confidence in hand independence takes time and patience. Let's get there, step-by-step. First, we'll use our scales to practice some hand-independence exercises.

Hand-Independence Drills: C Major

Hand-Independence Drills: F Major

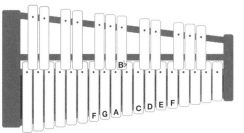

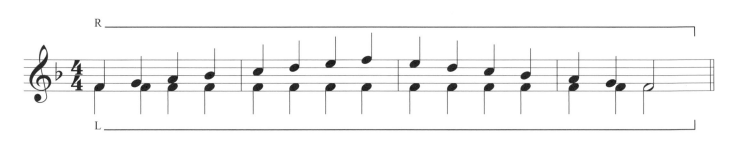

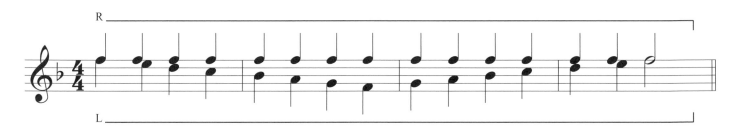

Hand-Independence Drills: G Major

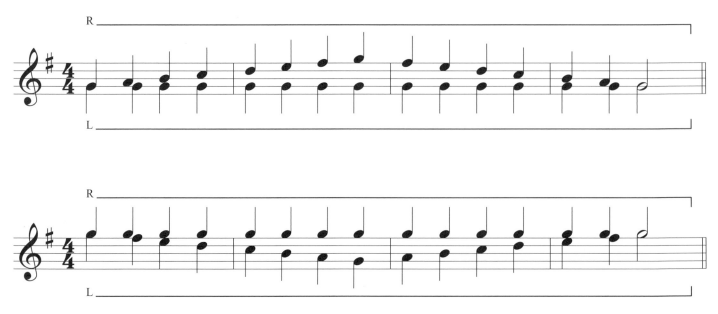

HAND INDEPENDENCE IN PERFORMANCE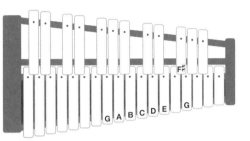

Up and Down the Ladder

Morning Bells

Twirling Kites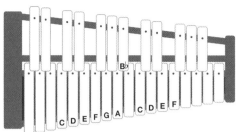

EVELYN'S TIPS

- In "Twirling Kites," the hands alternate roles more quickly. Break the piece down into measure-long chunks, slowly putting the chunks together as you grow in confidence.
- Once you are confident with the hand-independence technique in these three pieces, bring them to life with your own dynamics.

HAND DAMPENING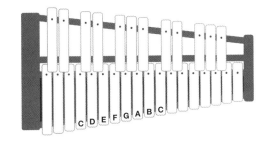

You will have noticed that the glockenspiel is wonderfully resonant. The sound of one note often overlaps with another or even resonates over a rest.

Sometimes, we need to control this resonance. We do so through the technique of **hand dampening**, which is where we stop a note from resonating. To do this, we place a hand on a glockenspiel bar after it has been struck. Hand dampening is an extension of our hand-independence technique; usually, one hand will be striking a glockenspiel bar with a mallet while the other simultaneously dampens a previously struck bar.

Hand-Dampening Practice: C Major

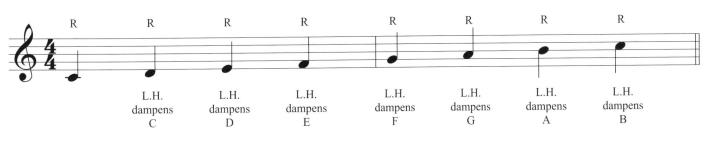

HAND-DAMPENING DRILLS

Hand-Dampening Practice: F Major

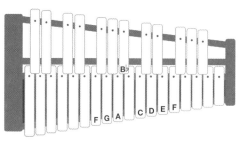

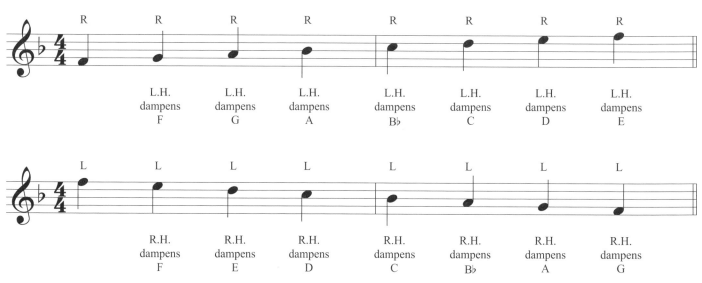

Hand-Dampening Practice: G Major

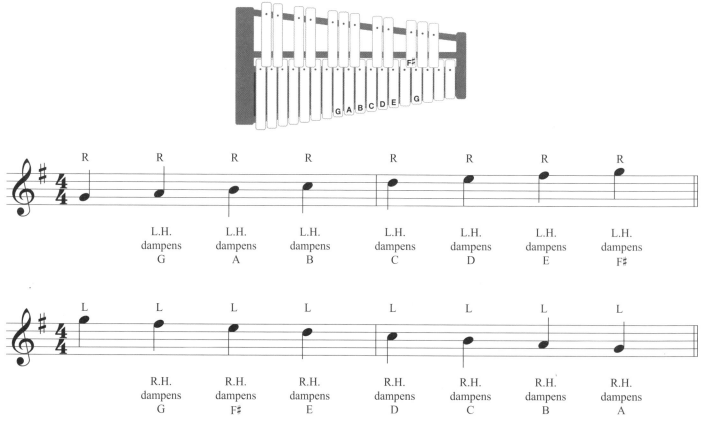

Hand Dampening Practice (Left Hand): C Major

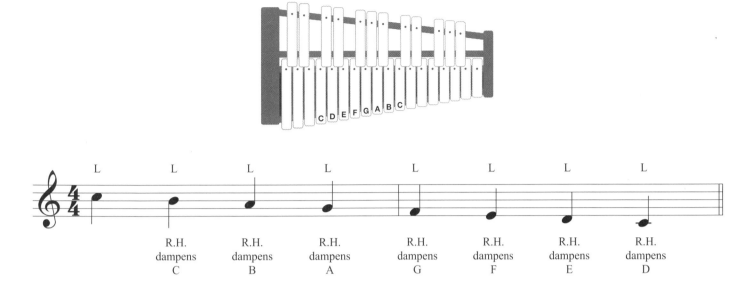

L   L   L   L   L   L   L   L

R.H. dampens C   R.H. dampens B   R.H. dampens A   R.H. dampens G   R.H. dampens F   R.H. dampens E   R.H. dampens D

HAND DAMPENING IN PERFORMANCE

Now, let's revisit a piece we learned earlier but use hand dampening.

Helping Hand (Dampening)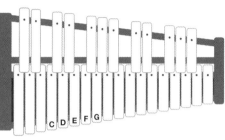

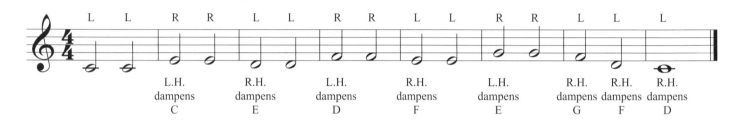

SOUND EFFECTS

It's great to let our imagination fly and explore the different types of sound that our instrument is able to produce.

CREATING NEW SOUNDS

Here are some ways to create exciting new **timbres** (types of sound) on your glockenspiel.

1. Use **mallets made from different materials**.

2. **Strike with the shaft of your mallets**, rather than the head.

3. Explore **striking different areas of the bars** to create new sounds.

4. Experiment with the **dead stroke**, which is where we prevent the bars from resonating.

Let's begin by exploring sound effects using scales that we know. Try each of the methods above on your F and G major scales. Have fun and experiment before moving onto the sound-effect pieces over the next few pages.

Sounds in F Major

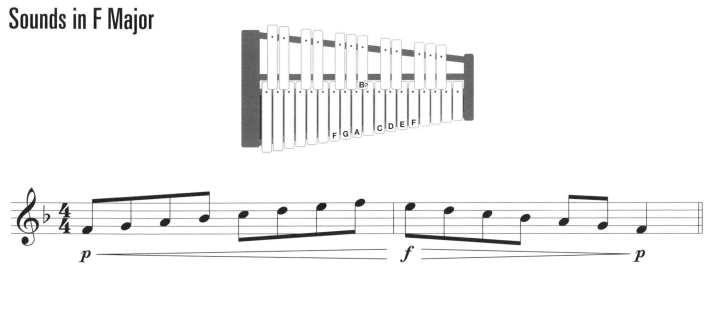

Sounds in G Major

SOUND EFFECTS IN PERFORMANCE

1. Get to know the piece by learning the notes and rhythms using your usual mallet technique.

2. Now, play the piece using a different mallet type in each hand.

3. Finally, try the "dead stroke" in the left hand, combined with a soft mallet type in the right hand.

If you only have one type of mallet, just have fun exploring the other types of sound effects we have learned together. Use your imagination to make the music fun and engaging!

Make Your Mind Up

DUET PLAYING

A **duet** is a piece specifically written for two players. This duet has been written so that two glockenspiel performers can make music together. If you don't have a glockenspiel duet partner, one of the parts can be played on the piano or you can play along with the online audio.

Sweet Dreams

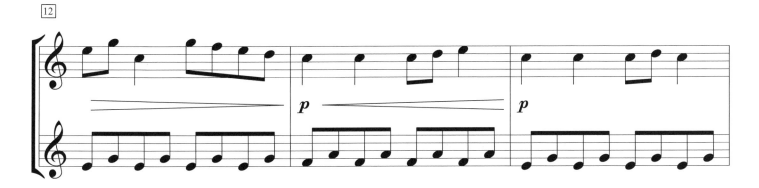

EVELYN'S TIPS

- It's a great idea for you and your duet partner to learn both parts of a duet. That way, you'll have a real understanding of what each other is playing and will be able to perform beautifully as a team.
- Experiment with enhancing the music with sound effects. Try choosing a section of the piece to play using just the shaft of the mallets. Striking close to the rubber peg points will create a "distant" sound, appropriate for the music's title. How can you both bring the piece to life by using lots of different types of sound?

PUTTING IT ALL TOGETHER

This duet combines a rich range of notes, note values, expressive markings, and techniques. You have everything you need to perform this with confidence and musicality. Be sure to work together as a team and experiment with different sound effects to enhance your interpretation of the music. If you don't have a glockenspiel duet partner, one of the parts can be played on the piano or you can play along with the online audio.

Letting Go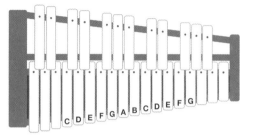

CONGRATULATIONS!

Many congratulations on completing the *Hal Leonard Glockenspiel Method*. Everything you have learned so far will provide a strong foundation upon which to continue studying this wonderful instrument. I hope you will enjoy many years of rewarding music-making with the glockenspiel and try out lots of other percussion instruments, too. There is an exciting world of sound out there to explore. So, good luck and keep experimenting!

Evelyn Glennie

HAL LEONARD DRUM & PERCUSSION METHODS

HAL LEONARD CAJON METHOD
by Paul Jennings

This beginner's guide for anyone learning to play the cajon takes you through the basics of the instrument and its techniques with dozens of exercises and over 30 grooves from many genres including rock, Latin, blues, jazz, flamenco, funk, and more. There are also more advanced techniques in the final chapter that include how to change the pitch with your foot, playing with brushes, and playing rolls with your fingers.

00138215 Book/Online Video $14.99

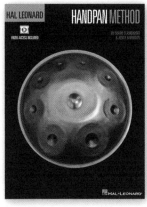

HAL LEONARD HANDPAN METHOD
by Mark D'Ambrosio & Jenny Robinson

The *Hal Leonard Handpan Method* is written for a broad range of skill levels. Beginners will find the introductory material and exercises necessary to develop their touch and technical skill, while the advanced player will find instructions on how to execute high-level techniques, create sophisticated sounds, and build complex patterns. The information, techniques, and theory presented in this book are designed to be flexible, and can be adapted to work on your instrument, no matter the scale or number of notes. The price of this book includes access to videos online, for download or streaming, using the unique code included with each purchase.

00288061 Book/Online Video $14.99

HAL LEONARD DJEMBE METHOD
by Paul Jennings

This beginner's guide takes you through the basics of the instrument and its techniques. The accompanying online videos include demonstrations of many examples in the book. Topics covered include: notation • bass and slap tone exercises • three- and four-tone exercises • basic rhythms • traditional djembe rhythms • modern techniques • and much more.

00145559 Book/Online Video $14.99

HAL LEONARD SNARE DRUM METHOD
by Rick Mattingly

Geared toward beginning band and orchestra students, this modern, musical approach to learning snare drum includes play-along audio files that feature full concert band recordings of band arrangements and classic marches with complete drum parts that allow the beginning drummer to apply the book's lessons in a realistic way.

06620059 Book/Online Audio...........................$14.99

HAL LEONARD DRUMSET METHOD
by Kennan Wylie with Gregg Bissonette

Lessons in Book 1 include: drum setup & fundamentals • tuning & maintenance • basic music reading • grips & strokes • coordination & basic techniques • basic beats for many styles of music • 8th notes, 16th notes, dotted notes & triplets • drum fills • and more. Lessons in Book 2 include: limb independence • half-time grooves • syncopation • funk grooves • ghost notes • jazz drumming • chart reading • drum soloing • brush playing • and much more.

00209864 Book 1/Online Media.......................$17.99
00209865 Book 2/Online Media.......................$16.99
00209866 Books 1 & 2/
　　　　　Online Media, Comb-Bound............$27.50

HAL LEONARD STEELPAN METHOD
by Liam Teague

The *Hal Leonard Steelpan Method* is designed for anyone just learning to play the steelpan. This easy-to-use beginner's guide takes you through the basics of the instrument and its technique. It covers: stance • holding the mallets • types of strokes • tone production and volume control • stickings • rolls • scales • calypsos • many songs and exercises • basic music reading • steelpan anatomy and maintenance • steelpan history • and more.

00111629 Book/Online Audio...........................$14.99

HAL LEONARD DRUMS FOR KIDS

Drums for Kids is a fun, easy course that teaches children to play drumset faster than ever before. Popular songs will keep kids motivated, while the simple, easy-to-read page layouts ensure their attention remains focused on one concept at a time. The method can be used in combination with a drum teacher or parent.

00113420 Book/Online Audio...........................$14.99

See these and many other percussion titles at
halleonard.com